WELCOME TO THE U.S.A.

PUERTO RICO

Written by Ann Heinrichs Illustrated by Matt Kania
Content Adviser: Dr. Xavier F. Totti, Professor, Department of Latin American and Puerto Rican Studies, Lehman College, CUNY, Bronx, New York

Published in the United States of America by The Child's World®
PO Box 326 • Chanhassen, MN 55317-0326
800-599-READ • www.childsworld.com

Photo Credits

Cover: Getty Images/Stone/Mark Lewis; frontispiece: Bob Krist/Corbis.

Interior: AP/Wide World Photos: 10 (Herminio Rodriguez), 29 (Tomas van Houtryve); Tony Arruza/Corbis: 17, 22; Dave G. Houser/Corbis: 6, 18, 33; Stephanie Maze/Corbis: 25, 26; Kevin Schafer/Corbis: 9; travelandsports.com 2004: 13, 14, 21, 30, 34.

Acknowledgments

The Child's World®: Mary Berendes, Publishing Director

Editorial Directions, Inc.: E. Russell Primm, Editorial Director; Katie Marsico, Associate Editor; Judith Shiffer, Assistant Editor; Matt Messbarger, Editorial Assistant; Susan Hindman, Copy Editor; Melissa McDaniel, Proofreader; Kevin Cunningham, Peter Garnham, Matt Messbarger, Olivia Nellums, Chris Simms, Molly Symmonds, Katherine Trickle, Carl Stephen Wender, Fact Checkers; Tim Griffin/IndexServ, Indexer; Cian Loughlin O'Day, Photo Researcher and Editor

The Design Lab: Kathleen Petelinsek, Design; Julia Goozen, Art Production

Library of Congress Cataloging-in-Publication Data

Heinrichs, Ann.
Puerto Rico / by Ann Heinrichs ; cartography and illustrations by Matt Kania.
p. cm. — (Welcome to the U.S.A.)
Includes index.
ISBN 1-59296-493-1 (library bound : alk. paper) 1. Puerto Rico—Juvenile literature.
2. Puerto Rico—Geography—Juvenile literature. I. Kania, Matt. II. Title.
F1958.3.H45 2005
917.295—dc22 2005011364

Ann Heinrichs is the author of more than 100 books for children and young adults. She has also enjoyed successful careers as a children's book editor and an advertising copywriter. Ann grew up in Fort Smith, Arkansas, and lives in Chicago, Illinois.

About the Author
Ann Heinrichs

Matt Kania loves maps and, as a kid, dreamed of making them. In school he studied geography and cartography, and today he makes maps for a living. Matt's favorite thing about drawing maps is learning about the places they represent. Many of the maps he has created can be found in books, magazines, videos, Web sites, and public places.

About the Map Illustrator
Matt Kania

On the cover: El Morro is just one of Puerto Rico's many old forts.

On page one: Watch the water dance through the lights of a fountain at Plaza la Delicias.

OUR PUERTO RICO TRIP

FOR MORE INFORMATION

Puerto Rico's Nickname: Isle of Enchantment

Are you ready to explore Puerto Rico? Just look what's in store for you!

You'll visit **plantations** and forts. You'll see where Puerto Rico's early peoples played ball. You'll enjoy lots of colorful festivals. You'll swim among tiny sea creatures that glow. You'll hike through a **rain forest.** And you'll explore some spooky caves!

There's much more to discover, so buckle up. We're off to Puerto Rico!

WELCOME TO PUERTO RICO

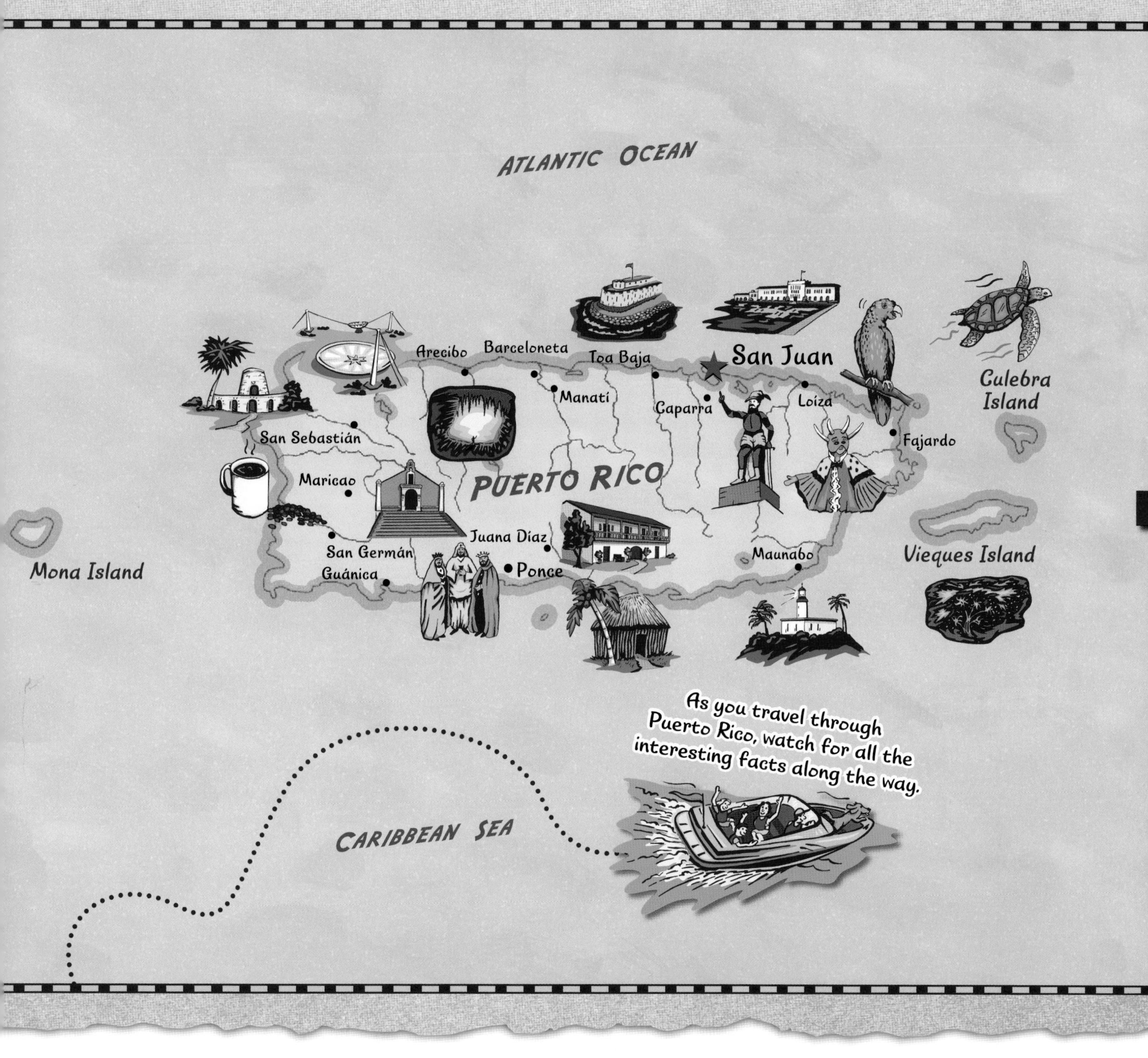

ATLANTIC OCEAN
Arecibo
Barceloneta
Toa Baja
San Juan
Manatí
Caparra
Loíza
Culebra Island
Fajardo
San Sebastián
PUERTO RICO
Maricao
Juana Díaz
San Germán
Guánica
Ponce
Maunabo
Vieques Island
Mona Island
As you travel through Puerto Rico, watch for all the interesting facts along the way.
CARIBBEAN SEA

Scared of the dark? Then bring a flashlight to Rio Camuy Cave Park!

Exploring Río Camuy Cave Park

You wander down the leafy green path. At last, you enter a spectacular cave. Its sparkling rock formations take your breath away!

You're exploring Río Camuy Cave Park. It's in the hills southwest of Arecibo.

Puerto Rico lies southeast of Florida. To the north is the Atlantic Ocean. To the south is the Caribbean Sea.

Puerto Rico's biggest cities are near the coast. Miles of sandy beaches line the coasts. Palm trees wave in the warm breezes there.

Away from the coast, the land becomes hilly. Rugged mountains run across central Puerto Rico. The highest mountain range is the Cordillera Central.

Puerto Rico's mountains have many sinkholes. These are deep holes in a region that contains limestone rock.

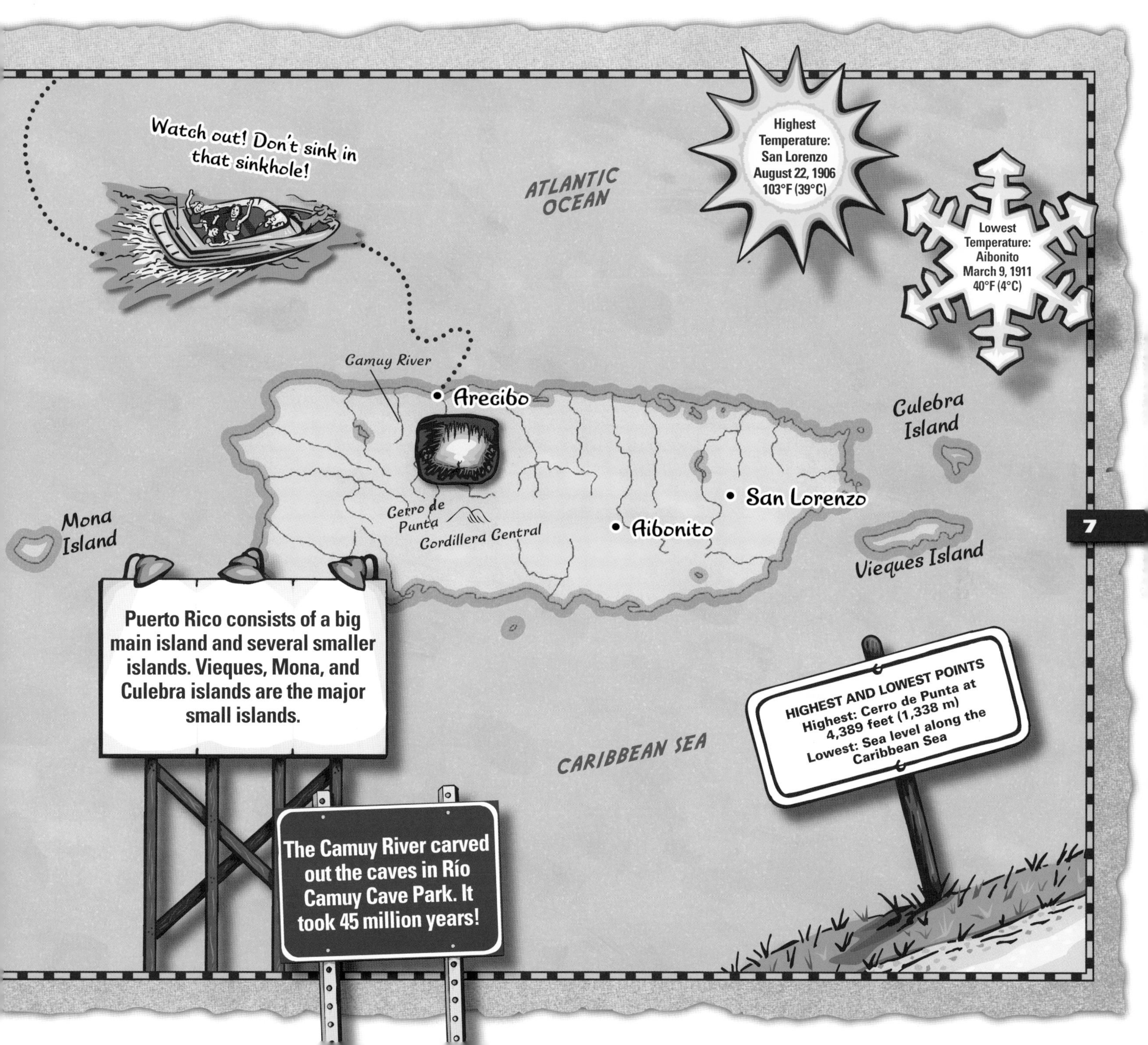

Watch out! Don't sink in that sinkhole!
ATLANTIC OCEAN
Highest Temperature: San Lorenzo August 22, 1906 103°F (39°C)
Lowest Temperature: Aibonito March 9, 1911 40°F (4°C)
Camuy River
Arecibo
Culebra Island
San Lorenzo
Aibonito
Cerro de Punta
Cordillera Central
Mona Island
Vieques Island
Puerto Rico consists of a big main island and several smaller islands. Vieques, Mona, and Culebra islands are the major small islands.
HIGHEST AND LOWEST POINTS
Highest: Cerro de Punta at 4,389 feet (1,338 m)
Lowest: Sea level along the Caribbean Sea
CARIBBEAN SEA
The Camuy River carved out the caves in Río Camuy Cave Park. It took 45 million years!

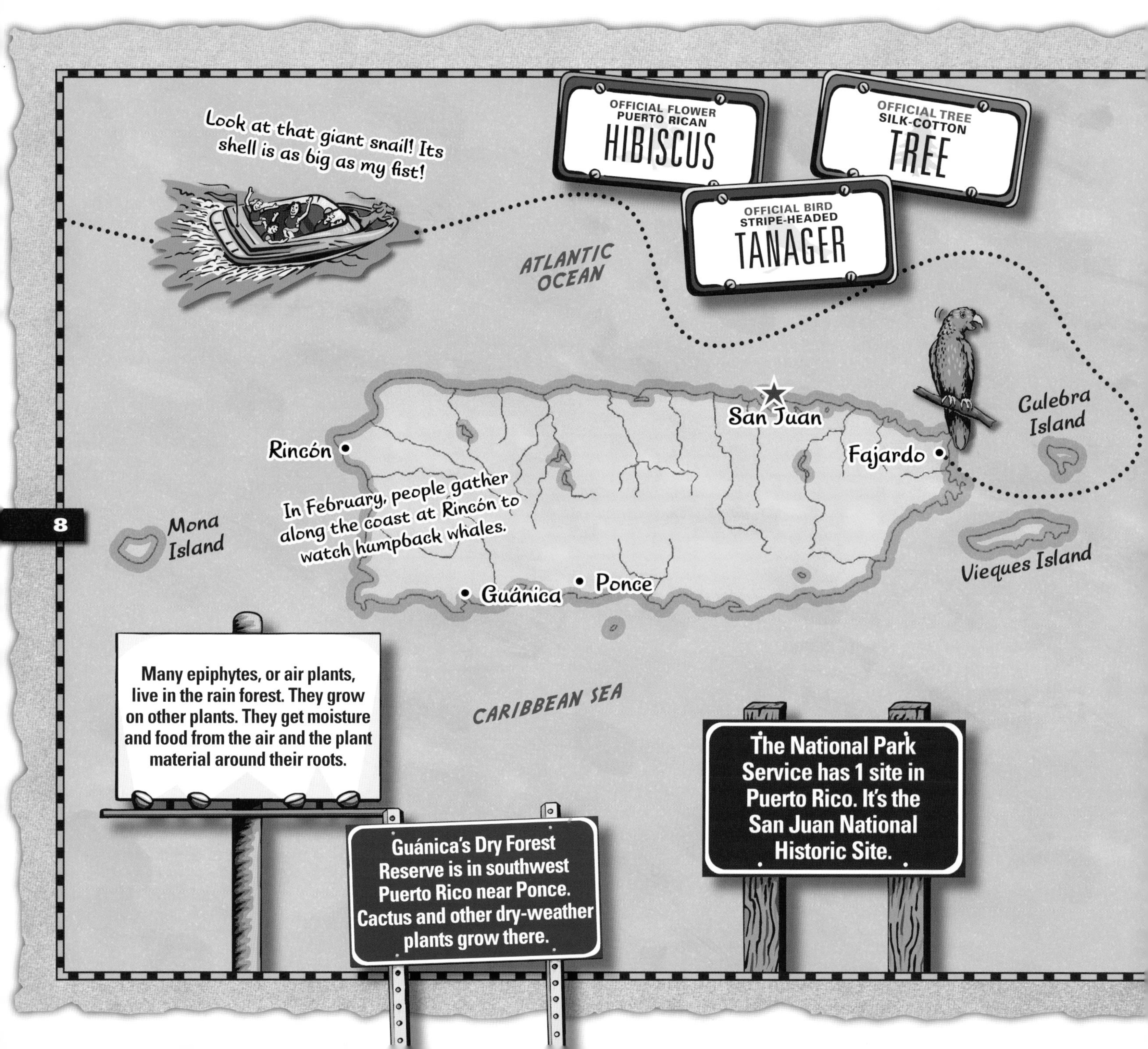

Look at that giant snail! Its shell is as big as my fist!
OFFICIAL FLOWER
PUERTO RICAN
HIBISCUS
OFFICIAL TREE
SILK-COTTON
TREE
OFFICIAL BIRD
STRIPE-HEADED
TANAGER
ATLANTIC OCEAN
San Juan
Rincón
Fajardo
Culebra Island
Mona Island
In February, people gather along the coast at Rincón to watch humpback whales.
Vieques Island
Guánica
Ponce
CARIBBEAN SEA
Many epiphytes, or air plants, live in the rain forest. They grow on other plants. They get moisture and food from the air and the plant material around their roots.
The National Park Service has 1 site in Puerto Rico. It's the San Juan National Historic Site.
Guánica's Dry Forest Reserve is in southwest Puerto Rico near Ponce. Cactus and other dry-weather plants grow there.

Wildlife in El Yunque Rain Forest

The mongoose was brought to Puerto Rico to control rats on the sugar plantations.

You brush past giant tree ferns. High overhead, leafy treetops block the sunlight. Thick vines hang down from the branches. A bright green parrot flits by. Suddenly, you hear a chirpy song. It's not a bird. It's a tiny tree frog, the *coquí*!

You're hiking through El Yunque rain forest. It's in the mountains west of Fajardo.

The small coquí makes a big noise noise! Visit El Yunque rain forest and listen for yourself!

Puerto Rico is home to many other animals. The long, slender mongoose feasts on snakes. Lots of bats live in the island's caves. Wild goats live on Mona Island. Giant iguanas live there, too!

The Puerto Rican parrot is one of the rarest birds in the world. Its call sounds like a bugle blaring loudly.

Get Glowing in Mosquito Bay!

Watch the water light up as you paddle! You're boating in Mosquito Bay!

Your boat glides along in the night. The water shimmers with a blue-green glow. Swish your fingers around in the water. It lights up like sparkling glitter!

You're cruising through Vieques Island's Mosquito Bay. Billions of tiny sea creatures live there. They light up when they're disturbed. Just try jumping in the water. You'll be dripping with sparkly water drops!

Mosquito Bay is also called Bioluminescent Bay. A bioluminescent creature is one that produces light. When's the best time to visit Mosquito Bay? On a cloudless night when the moon's not out!

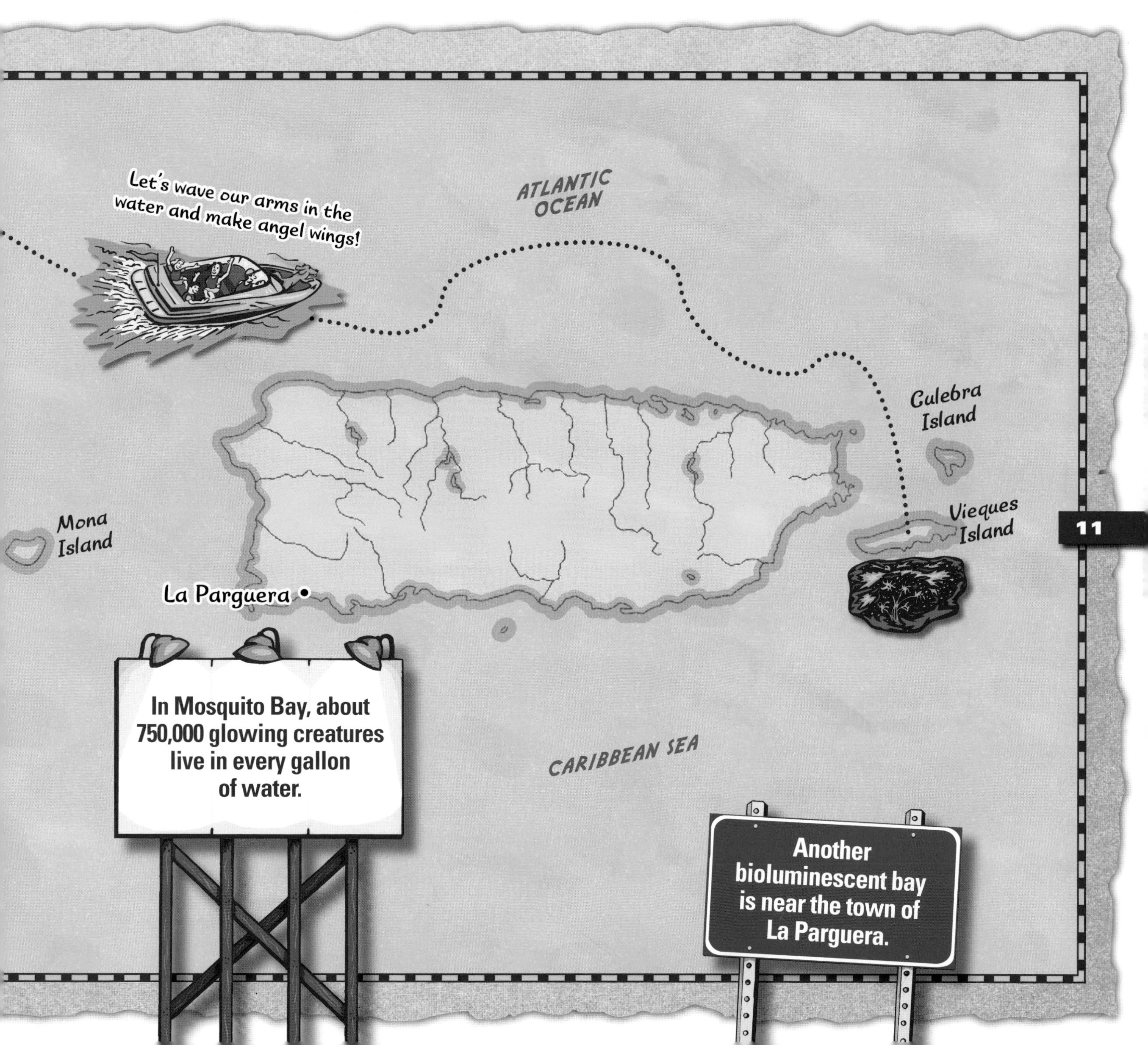
Let's wave our arms in the water and make angel wings!
ATLANTIC OCEAN
Culebra Island
Vieques Island
Mona Island
La Parguera
In Mosquito Bay, about 750,000 glowing creatures live in every gallon of water.
CARIBBEAN SEA
Another bioluminescent bay is near the town of La Parguera.

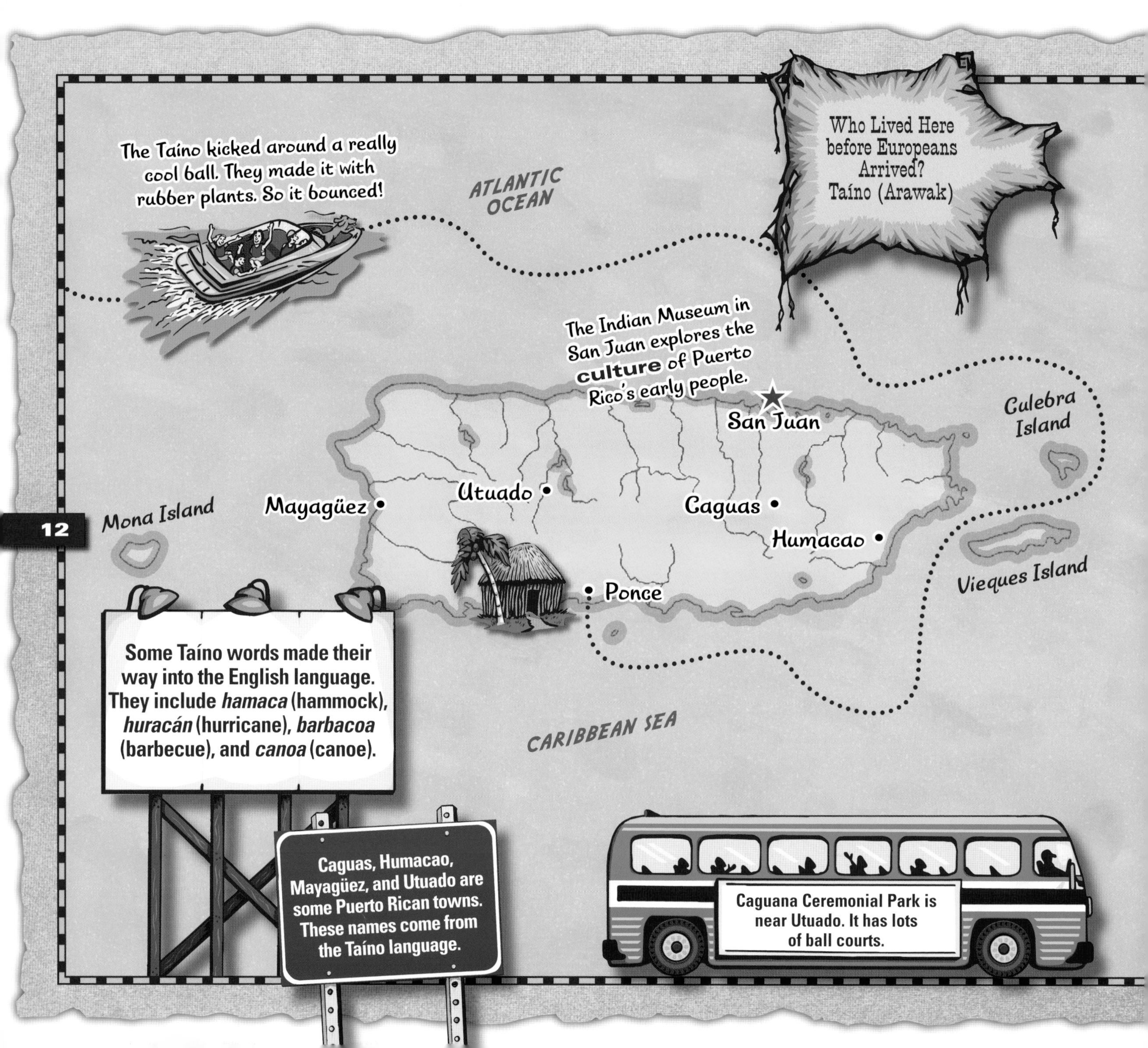

Who Lived Here before Europeans Arrived?
Taíno (Arawak)
The Taíno kicked around a really cool ball. They made it with rubber plants. So it bounced!
ATLANTIC OCEAN
The Indian Museum in San Juan explores the **culture** of Puerto Rico's early people.
San Juan
Culebra Island
Utuado
Mayagüez
Caguas
Humacao
Mona Island
Ponce
Vieques Island
CARIBBEAN SEA
Some Taíno words made their way into the English language. They include *hamaca* (hammock), *huracán* (hurricane), *barbacoa* (barbecue), and *canoa* (canoe).
Caguas, Humacao, Mayagüez, and Utuado are some Puerto Rican towns. These names come from the Taíno language.
Caguana Ceremonial Park is near Utuado. It has lots of ball courts.
12

Tibes Indian Ceremonial Center

How did Puerto Rico's early people live? Just visit Tibes Indian Ceremonial Center near Ponce. It features a rebuilt Taíno village. The Taíno people occupied Tibes more than 1,000 years ago. They called their homeland Boriquén, or Borinquen.

You'll see Taíno *bohíos*, or thatched-roof huts. You'll also see *bayetes*, or ball courts. People played a game like soccer there. Stones outline the borders of the courts. Some stones have petroglyphs, or carved pictures.

How did people in Puerto Rico live 1,000 years ago? Explore Tibes Indian Ceremonial Center to find out.

Christopher Columbus sailed to Puerto Rico in 1493. He claimed this land for Spain. He named it San Juan Bautista. That's Spanish for "Saint John the Baptist."

The Taíno slept in hanging woven nets called *hamacas*.

Ponce de León and Caparra

Walk in the footsteps of Puerto Rico's 1st Spanish governor at Caparra.

Stroll around Caparra. It doesn't look like much today. But it was Puerto Rico's first Spanish settlement. Juan Ponce de León arrived there in 1508. He met the Taíno chief Agueybana. The chief showed him gold from a nearby river.

Ponce de León established a plantation at Caparra. He became Puerto Rico's first Spanish governor. Later, more Spanish **colonists** arrived. They set up farms, forts, and towns. Some hunted for gold, too.

The Spaniards made the Taíno work as slaves. Many Taíno were killed. Even more died of diseases they caught from the Spaniards. Then Africans were brought in as slaves. They had hard lives, too.

The 1st African slaves arrived in Puerto Rico in 1513.

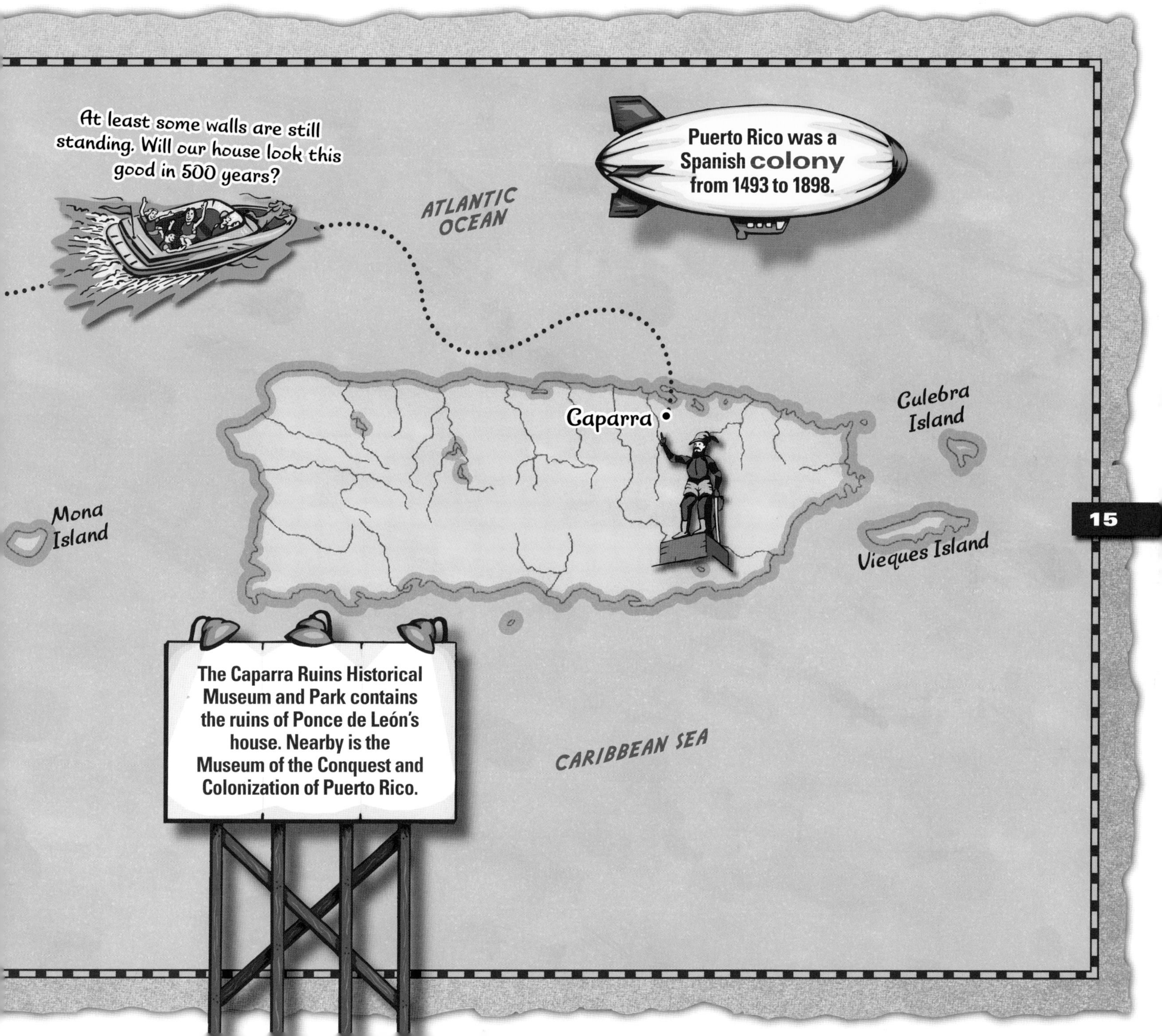
At least some walls are still standing. Will our house look this good in 500 years?
Puerto Rico was a Spanish colony from 1493 to 1898.
ATLANTIC OCEAN
Caparra
Culebra Island
Mona Island
Vieques Island
The Caparra Ruins Historical Museum and Park contains the ruins of Ponce de León's house. Nearby is the Museum of the Conquest and Colonization of Puerto Rico.
CARIBBEAN SEA

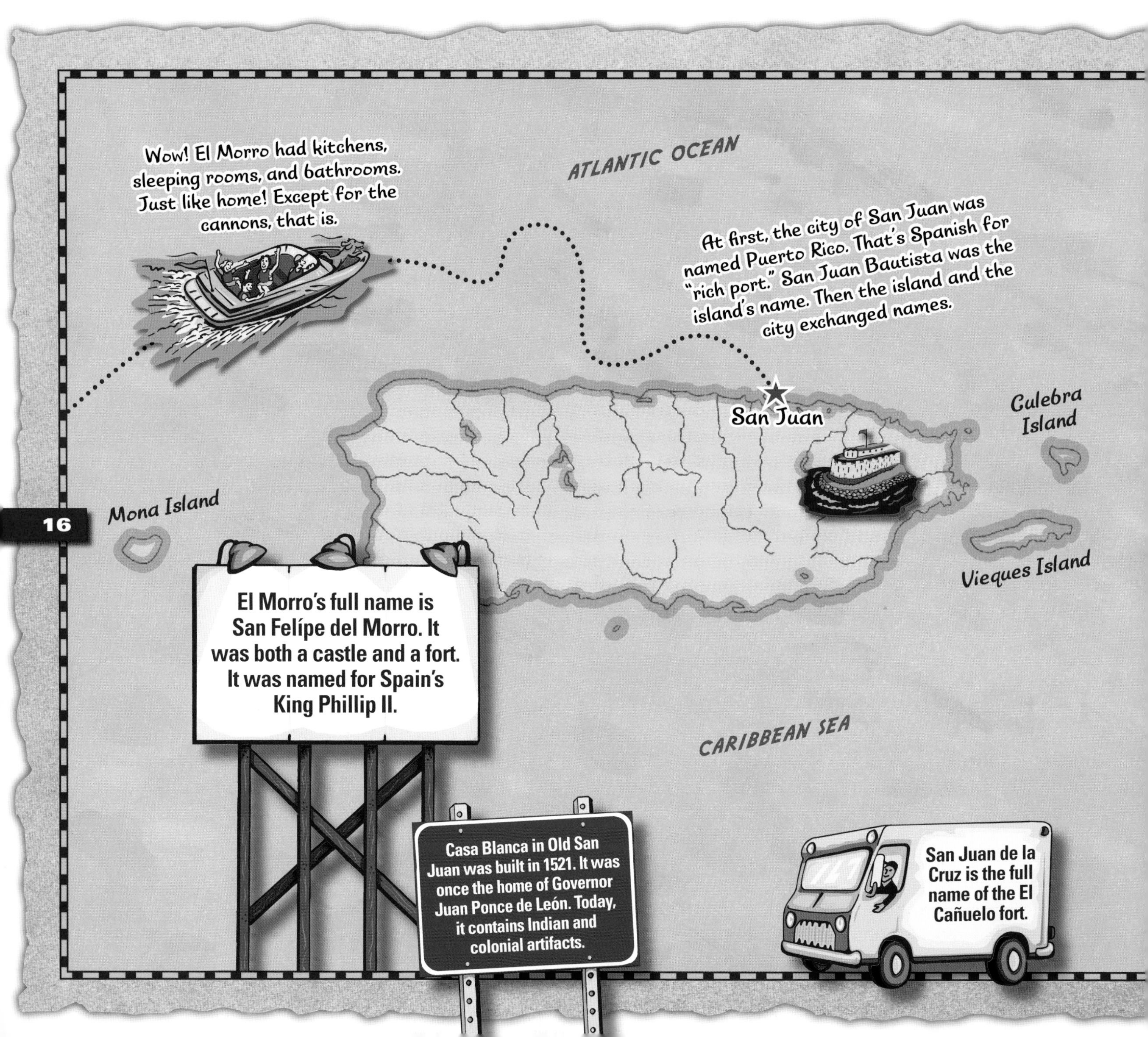

Wow! El Morro had kitchens, sleeping rooms, and bathrooms. Just like home! Except for the cannons, that is.
ATLANTIC OCEAN
At first, the city of San Juan was named Puerto Rico. That's Spanish for "rich port." San Juan Bautista was the island's name. Then the island and the city exchanged names.
San Juan
Culebra Island
Mona Island
Vieques Island
El Morro's full name is San Felípe del Morro. It was both a castle and a fort. It was named for Spain's King Phillip II.
CARIBBEAN SEA
Casa Blanca in Old San Juan was built in 1521. It was once the home of Governor Juan Ponce de León. Today, it contains Indian and colonial artifacts.
San Juan de la Cruz is the full name of the El Cañuelo fort.

Strolling through Old San Juan

The massive fort looks out over the sea. It's called El Morro. Spaniards built it to guard San Juan from attacks by sea. The fort's cannons could destroy enemy ships.

San Juan became the capital city in 1521. Now you can stroll through the city's old section. There you'll see many buildings from colonial times.

El Morro was not the city's only fort. San Cristóbal and El Cañuelo are two others. San Juan Cathedral stands in the old city, too. The body of Ponce de León rests there.

How strong were the forts at Old San Juan? You can still explore them almost 500 years later!

El Morro's walls are 18 feet (5 m) thick!

Hacienda Buena Vista Plantation

Farm animals roam around the grounds. There are slaves' quarters and horse stalls. Inside the mill, big machines are clanking. Take a trail through the forest. A sparkling waterfall rushes down the rocks. The water power runs the mill's machines.

You're touring Hacienda Buena Vista plantation. It's in the hills north of Ponce. Hacienda Buena Vista was a coffee plantation. The mill processed the coffee beans. It also ground corn into cornmeal.

Sugarcane was also an important crop by the 1800s. Thousands of slaves worked on Puerto Rico's sugar plantations.

What was life like on a coffee plantation? Tour Hacienda Buena Vista and find out!

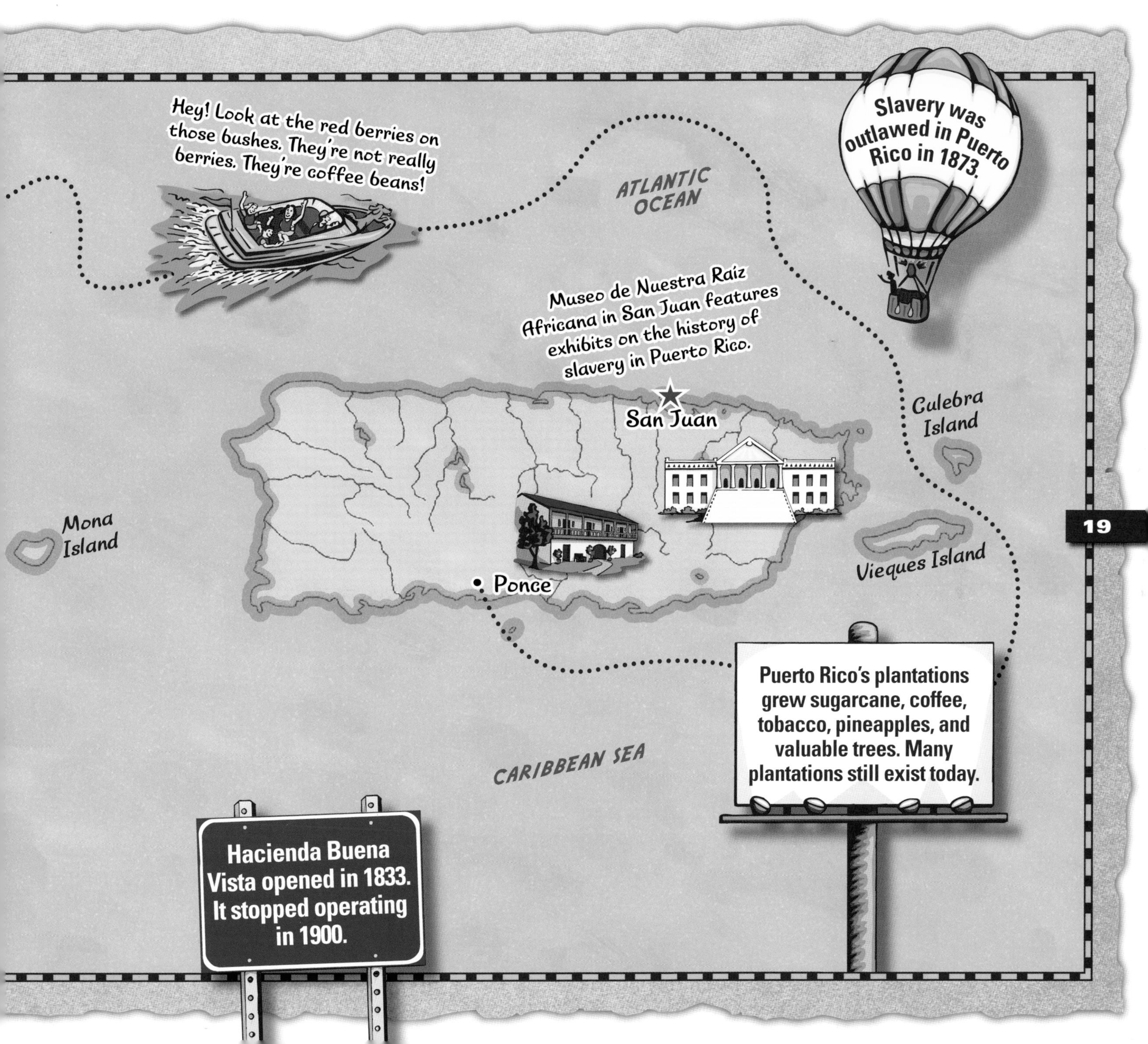
Hey! Look at the red berries on those bushes. They're not really berries. They're coffee beans!
Slavery was outlawed in Puerto Rico in 1873.
ATLANTIC OCEAN
Museo de Nuestra Raíz Africana in San Juan features exhibits on the history of slavery in Puerto Rico.
San Juan
Culebra Island
Mona Island
Vieques Island
Ponce
Puerto Rico's plantations grew sugarcane, coffee, tobacco, pineapples, and valuable trees. Many plantations still exist today.
CARIBBEAN SEA
Hacienda Buena Vista opened in 1833. It stopped operating in 1900.

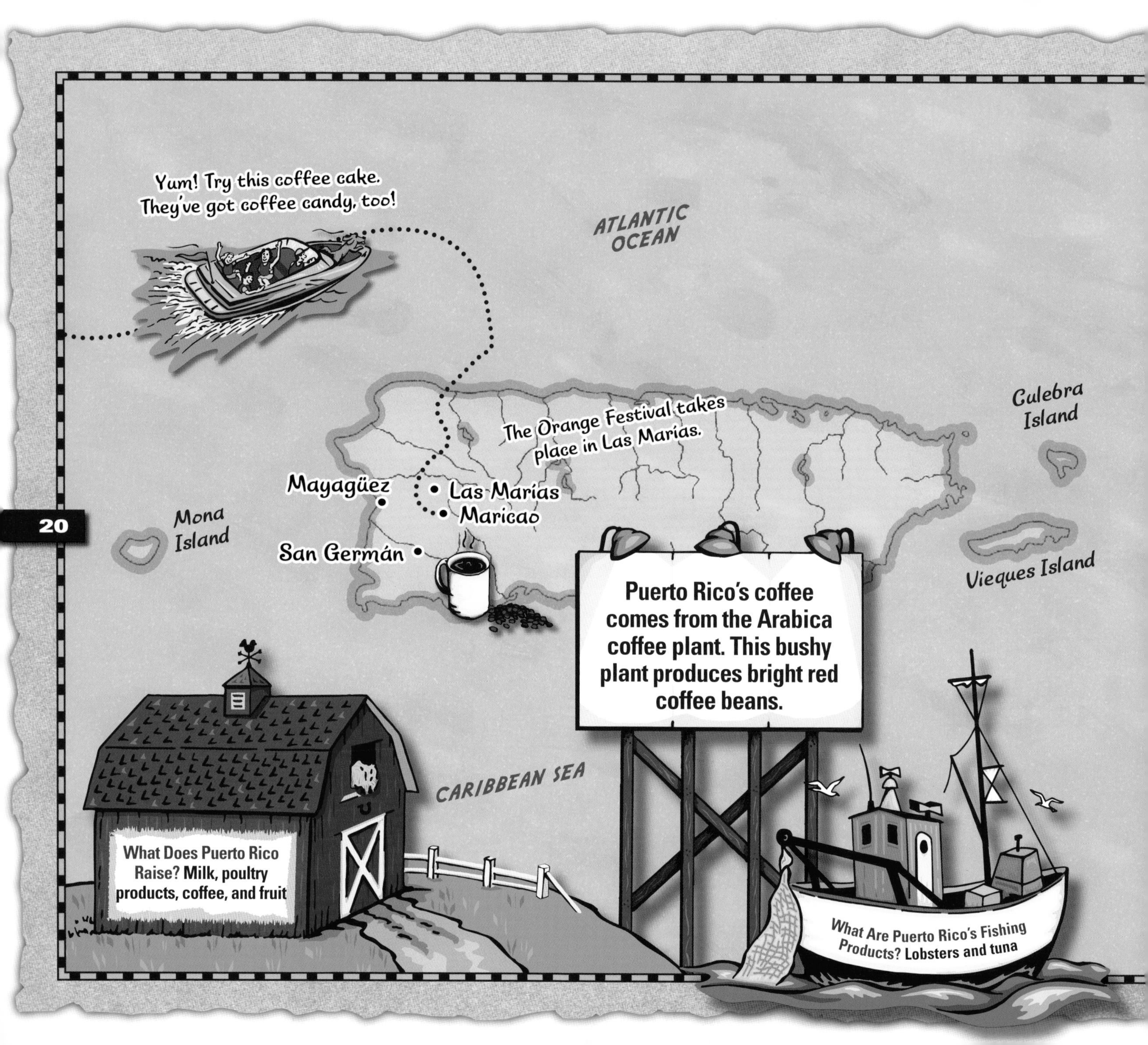

Yum! Try this coffee cake.
They've got coffee candy, too!
ATLANTIC OCEAN
Culebra Island
The Orange Festival takes place in Las Marías.
Mayagüez
Las Marías
Maricao
Mona Island
San Germán
Vieques Island
Puerto Rico's coffee comes from the Arabica coffee plant. This bushy plant produces bright red coffee beans.
CARIBBEAN SEA
What Does Puerto Rico Raise? Milk, poultry products, coffee, and fruit
What Are Puerto Rico's Fishing Products? Lobsters and tuna

Maricao's Coffee Harvest Festival

Mayagüez hosts the National Mango Fiesta.

Folk dancers whirl around in their colorful costumes. Food stalls sell delicious coffee desserts. Everywhere, the smell of coffee fills the air. It's the Coffee Harvest Festival!

Coffee was introduced in the 1700s. Today, it's Puerto Rico's major crop. Much of it grows in the western highlands.

Plantains are one of Puerto Rico's leading fruits. They're a type of banana. Bananas, pineapples, mangoes, and avocados are also important. Sugarcane is a valuable crop, too. Many farmers raise milk cows and beef cattle.

Do you smell coffee? You must be at Maricao's Coffee Harvest Festival!

San Germán holds a sugarcane festival every year.

Loíza's Saint James Festival

These colorful costumes are just part of the fun at the Saint James Festival in Loíza.

People are wearing baggy costumes. And their masks are a fright! They look like ugly monsters. Big fangs poke out of their fiery mouths. And long horns stick out from their heads!

You're watching the Saint James Festival in Loíza. It blends African and Spanish cultures. Many African slaves once lived in Loíza. Most residents today have African roots. The masks grew out of African **traditions.**

Religious festivals are common in Puerto Rico. Each town has a **patron saint.** The saint's feast day is a big event. Processions move through the plaza, or town square. Then everyone enjoys music, dancing, and food.

Puerto Rico's official languages are Spanish and English. But Spanish is the most widely spoken language.

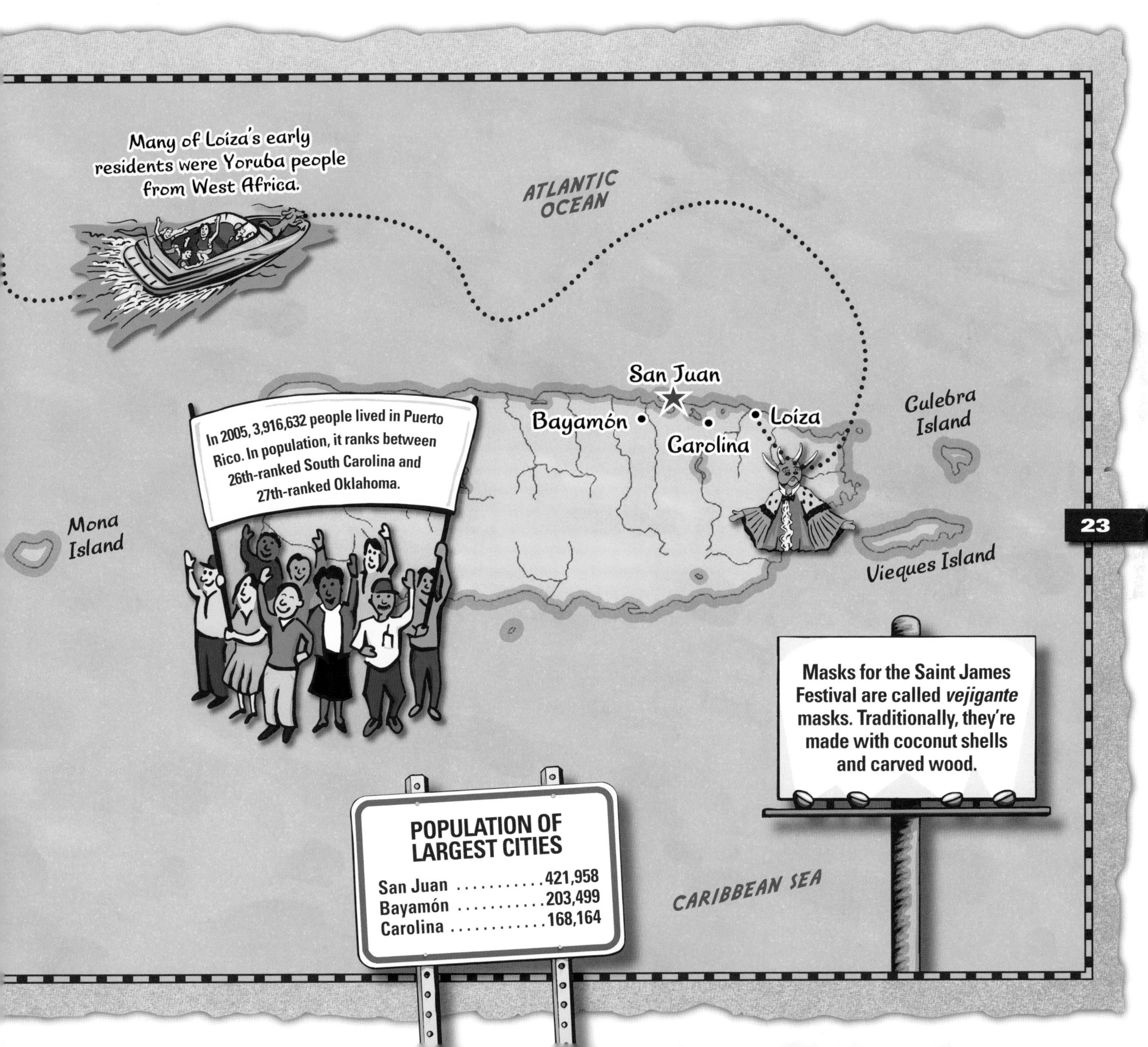
Many of Loíza's early residents were Yoruba people from West Africa.
ATLANTIC OCEAN
San Juan
Bayamón
Carolina
Loíza
Culebra Island
Vieques Island
Mona Island
In 2005, 3,916,632 people lived in Puerto Rico. In population, it ranks between 26th-ranked South Carolina and 27th-ranked Oklahoma.
Masks for the Saint James Festival are called *vejigante* masks. Traditionally, they're made with coconut shells and carved wood.
POPULATION OF LARGEST CITIES
San Juan 421,958
Bayamón 203,499
Carolina 168,164
CARIBBEAN SEA

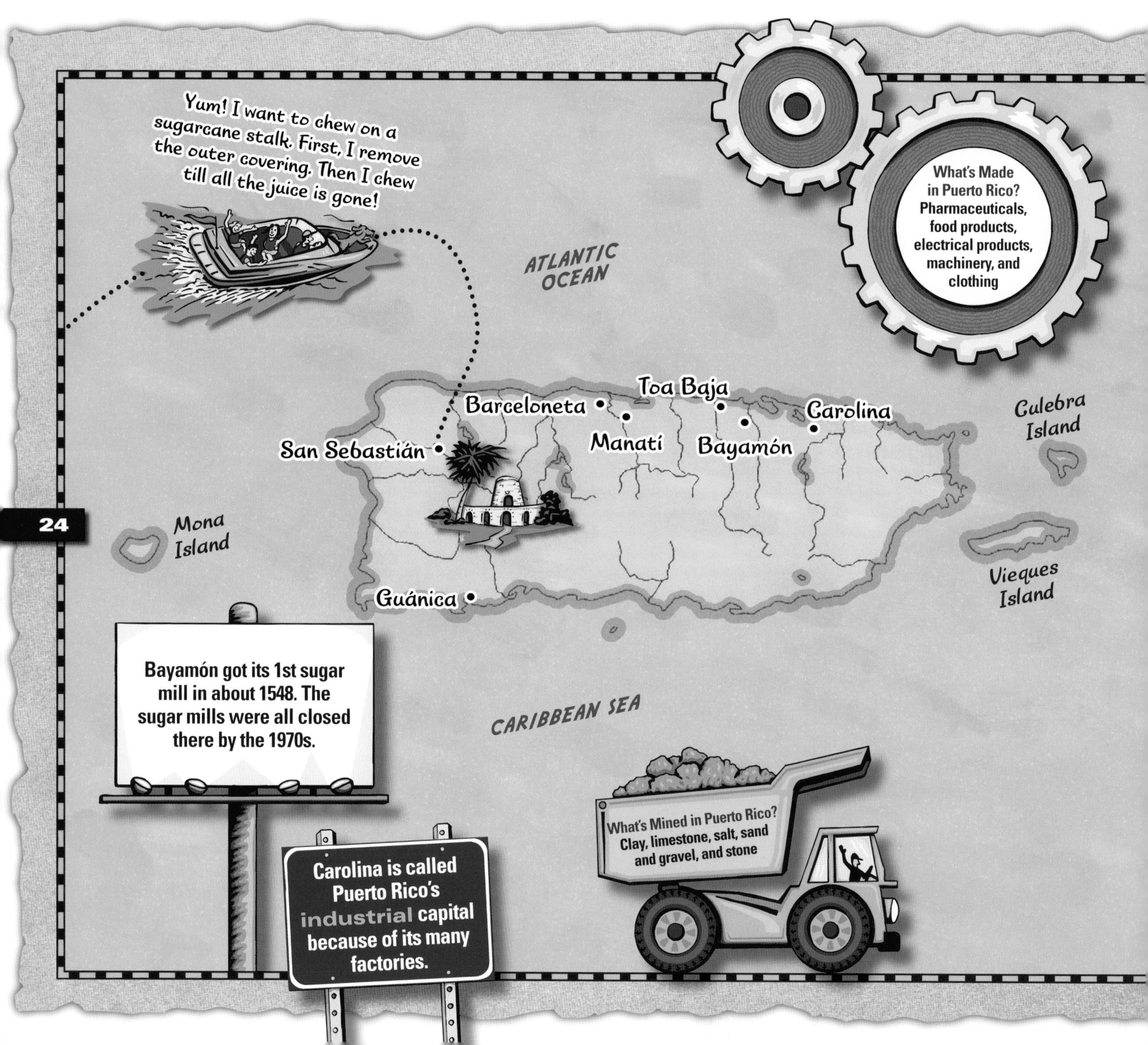

Yum! I want to chew on a sugarcane stalk. First, I remove the outer covering. Then I chew till all the juice is gone!
What's Made in Puerto Rico? Pharmaceuticals, food products, electrical products, machinery, and clothing
ATLANTIC OCEAN
Toa Baja
Barceloneta
Carolina
Culebra Island
Manatí
Bayamón
San Sebastián
Mona Island
Guánica
Vieques Island
Bayamón got its 1st sugar mill in about 1548. The sugar mills were all closed there by the 1970s.
CARIBBEAN SEA
What's Mined in Puerto Rico? Clay, limestone, salt, sand and gravel, and stone
Carolina is called Puerto Rico's industrial capital because of its many factories.

Sugar Mills, Old and New

Puerto Rican factories make medicines for many U.S. drug companies.

Drive across the countryside in Puerto Rico. Here and there, you see tall brick chimneys. They are the ruins of old sugar mills. Blazing furnaces provided heat to process the sugarcane. The chimneys belched out smoke from the fires.

You can tour Guánica's old sugar mill. It belonged to Hacienda Igualdad plantation. Manatí has an old mill, too. So do San Sebastián, Toa Baja, and Barceloneta.

Foods are valuable factory products in Puerto Rico. And sugar has been important for centuries. Sugar mills still turn sugarcane into sugar. Other factories make medicines, electrical equipment, and machines.

Do you have a sweet tooth? Stop by a Puerto Rican sugar plantation!

Tour La Fortaleza to see how Puerto Rico's governor lives.

La Fortaleza

La Fortaleza stands in Old San Juan. But is it a fort or a home? It's both. It was built as a fort in the 1500s. But it soon became the governor's **mansion.** Puerto Rico's governors still live and work there.

Puerto Rico passed to the United States in 1898. In 1952, it became a U.S. **commonwealth.** It formed a government with three branches. One branch makes laws. Its members meet in San Juan's capitol. Another branch carries out the laws. The governor heads this branch. Judges make up the third branch. They decide whether someone has broken the law.

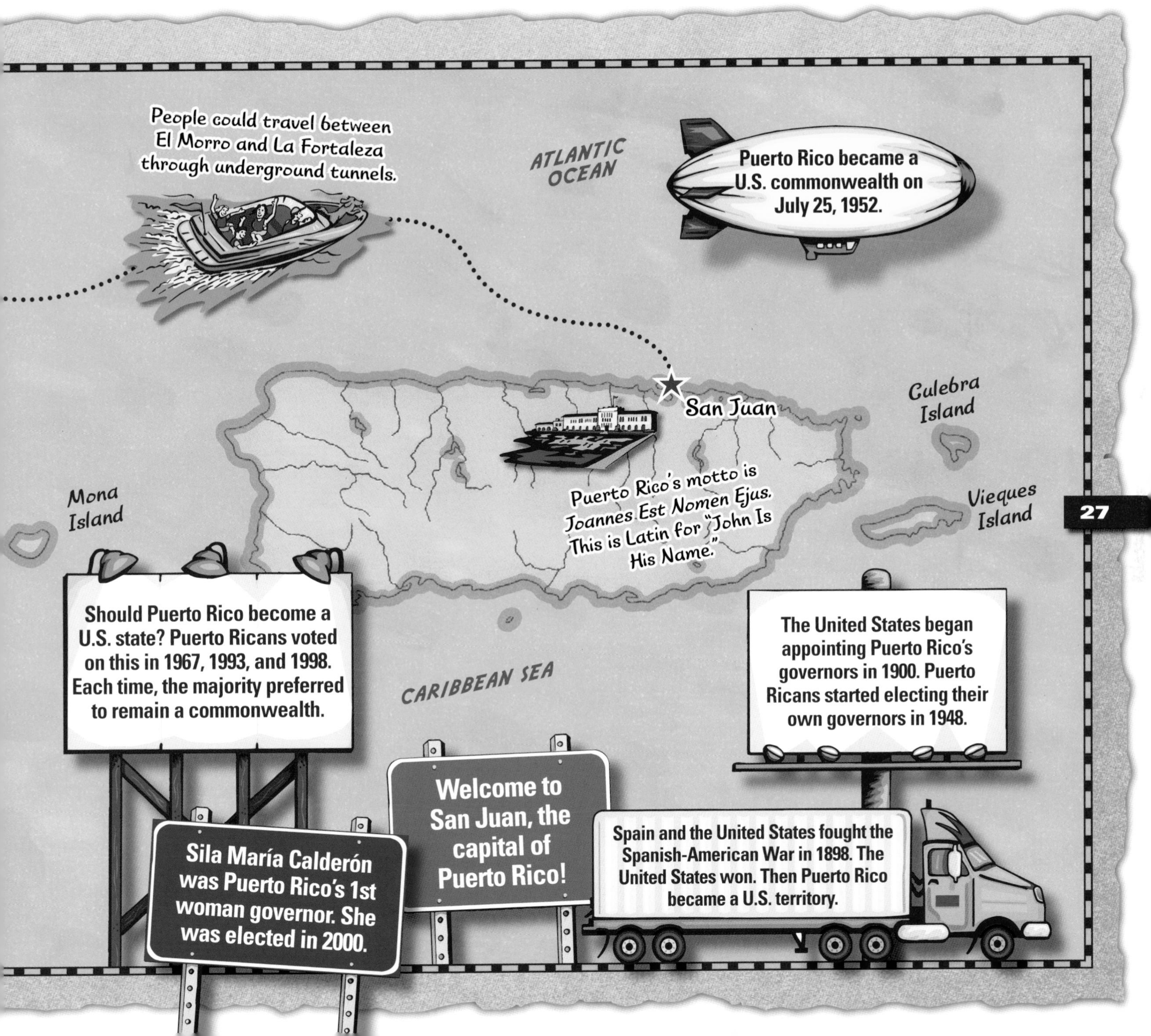

People could travel between El Morro and La Fortaleza through underground tunnels.
ATLANTIC OCEAN
Puerto Rico became a U.S. commonwealth on July 25, 1952.
San Juan
Culebra Island
Mona Island
Vieques Island
Puerto Rico's motto is Joannes Est Nomen Ejus. This is Latin for "John Is His Name."
Should Puerto Rico become a U.S. state? Puerto Ricans voted on this in 1967, 1993, and 1998. Each time, the majority preferred to remain a commonwealth.
CARIBBEAN SEA
The United States began appointing Puerto Rico's governors in 1900. Puerto Ricans started electing their own governors in 1948.
Welcome to San Juan, the capital of Puerto Rico!
Sila María Calderón was Puerto Rico's 1st woman governor. She was elected in 2000.
Spain and the United States fought the Spanish-American War in 1898. The United States won. Then Puerto Rico became a U.S. territory.

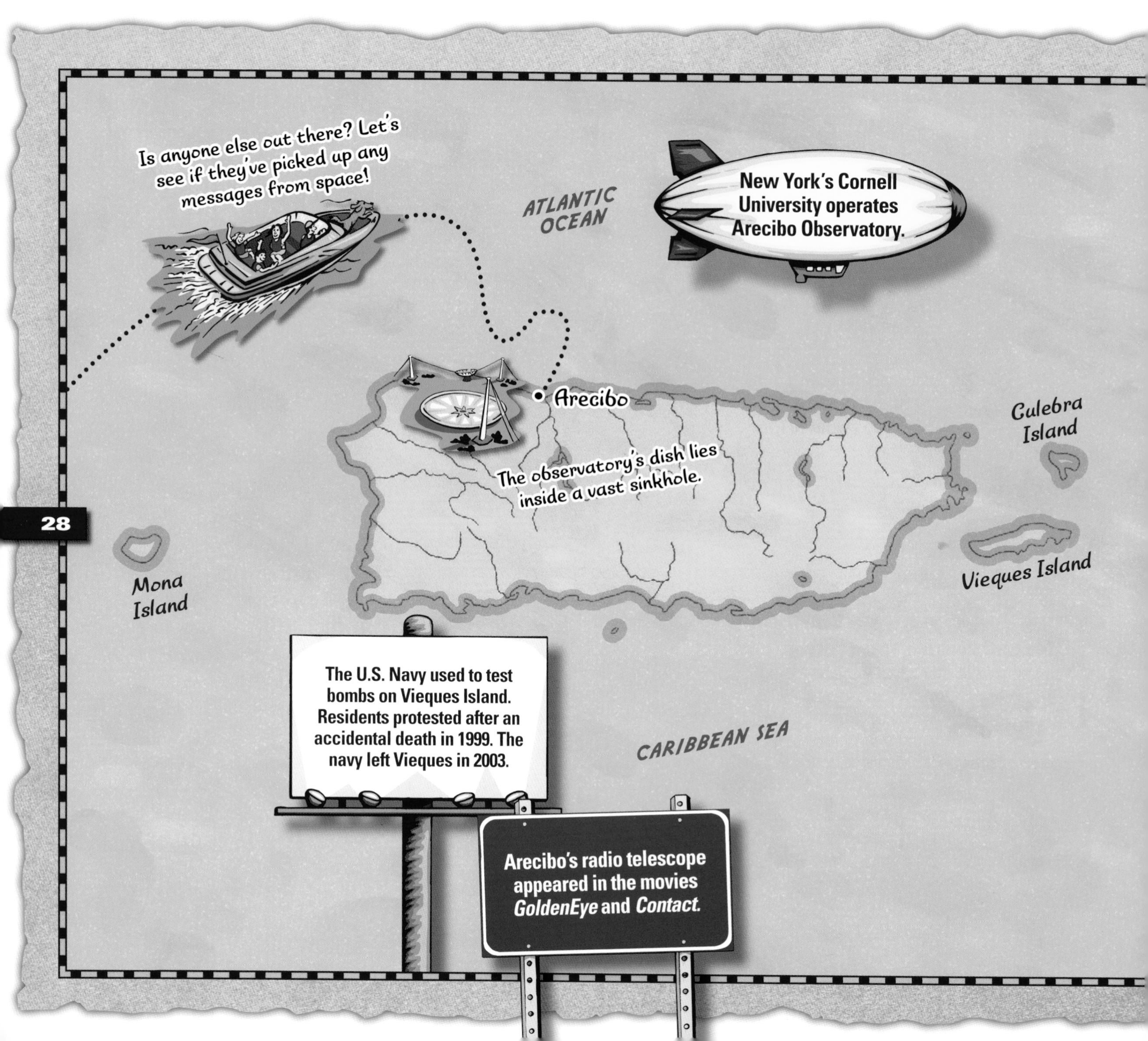
Is anyone else out there? Let's see if they've picked up any messages from space!
ATLANTIC OCEAN
New York's Cornell University operates Arecibo Observatory.
Arecibo
Culebra Island
The observatory's dish lies inside a vast sinkhole.
Mona Island
Vieques Island
The U.S. Navy used to test bombs on Vieques Island. Residents protested after an accidental death in 1999. The navy left Vieques in 2003.
CARIBBEAN SEA
Arecibo's radio telescope appeared in the movies *GoldenEye* and *Contact*.

Arecibo Observatory

Stand high on the platform. Look down at the big, curved dish. It could hold 26 football fields!

You're visiting Arecibo Observatory. It's up in the mountains south of Arecibo. It has a massive radio telescope.

The dish collects radio waves from space. Scientists study those waves. They learn about stars, planets, and other objects. Arecibo's scientists also work on the SETI project. *SETI* stands for "Search for **Extra-Terrestrial** Intelligence"!

U.S. organizations have many projects in Puerto Rico. Arecibo Observatory is one of them.

Like watching the stars? Scientists at Arecibo Observatory can see thousands of stars!

The Three Kings of Juana Díaz

Children are excited. Tomorrow is Three Kings Day—January 6. The Three Kings will come in the night.

The children fill a shoebox with grass. They slip the box under their beds. It's for the kings' hungry camels. In the morning, the grass is gone. The box is full of gifts!

Three Kings Day honors the three wise men. In Christian tradition, they visited the infant Jesus. In Juana Díaz, three men dress as the kings. They wear crowns and glittering robes. Children come and sit on their laps. They tell the kings what gifts they want!

Experience one of Puerto Rico's traditional celebrations on Three Kings Day.

January 6 is called the Feast of the Epiphany in much of the Christian world.

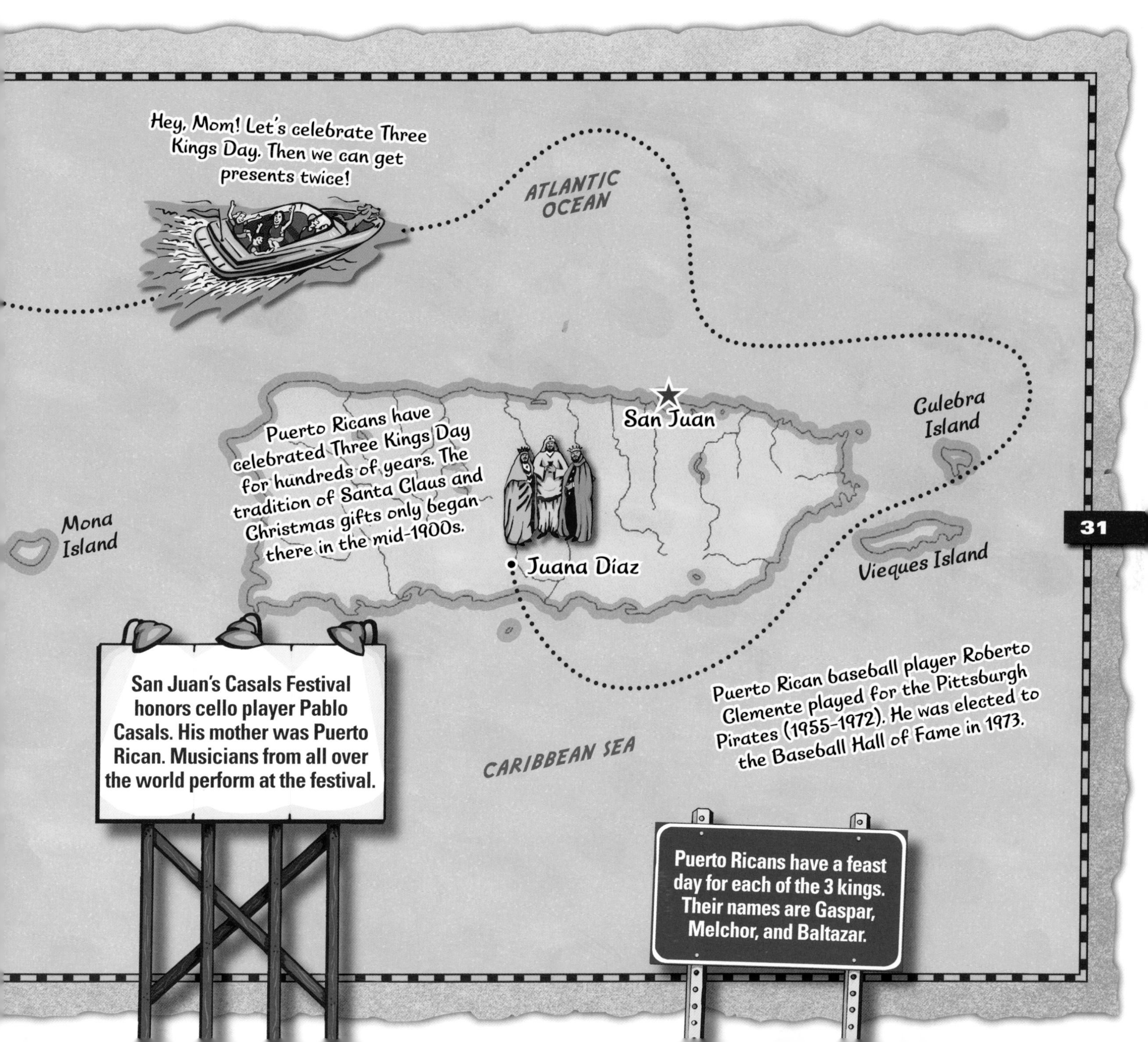
Hey, Mom! Let's celebrate Three Kings Day. Then we can get presents twice!
ATLANTIC OCEAN
Puerto Ricans have celebrated Three Kings Day for hundreds of years. The tradition of Santa Claus and Christmas gifts only began there in the mid-1900s.
San Juan
Culebra Island
Mona Island
Juana Díaz
Vieques Island
San Juan's Casals Festival honors cello player Pablo Casals. His mother was Puerto Rican. Musicians from all over the world perform at the festival.
Puerto Rican baseball player Roberto Clemente played for the Pittsburgh Pirates (1955–1972). He was elected to the Baseball Hall of Fame in 1973.
CARIBBEAN SEA
Puerto Ricans have a feast day for each of the 3 kings. Their names are Gaspar, Melchor, and Baltazar.

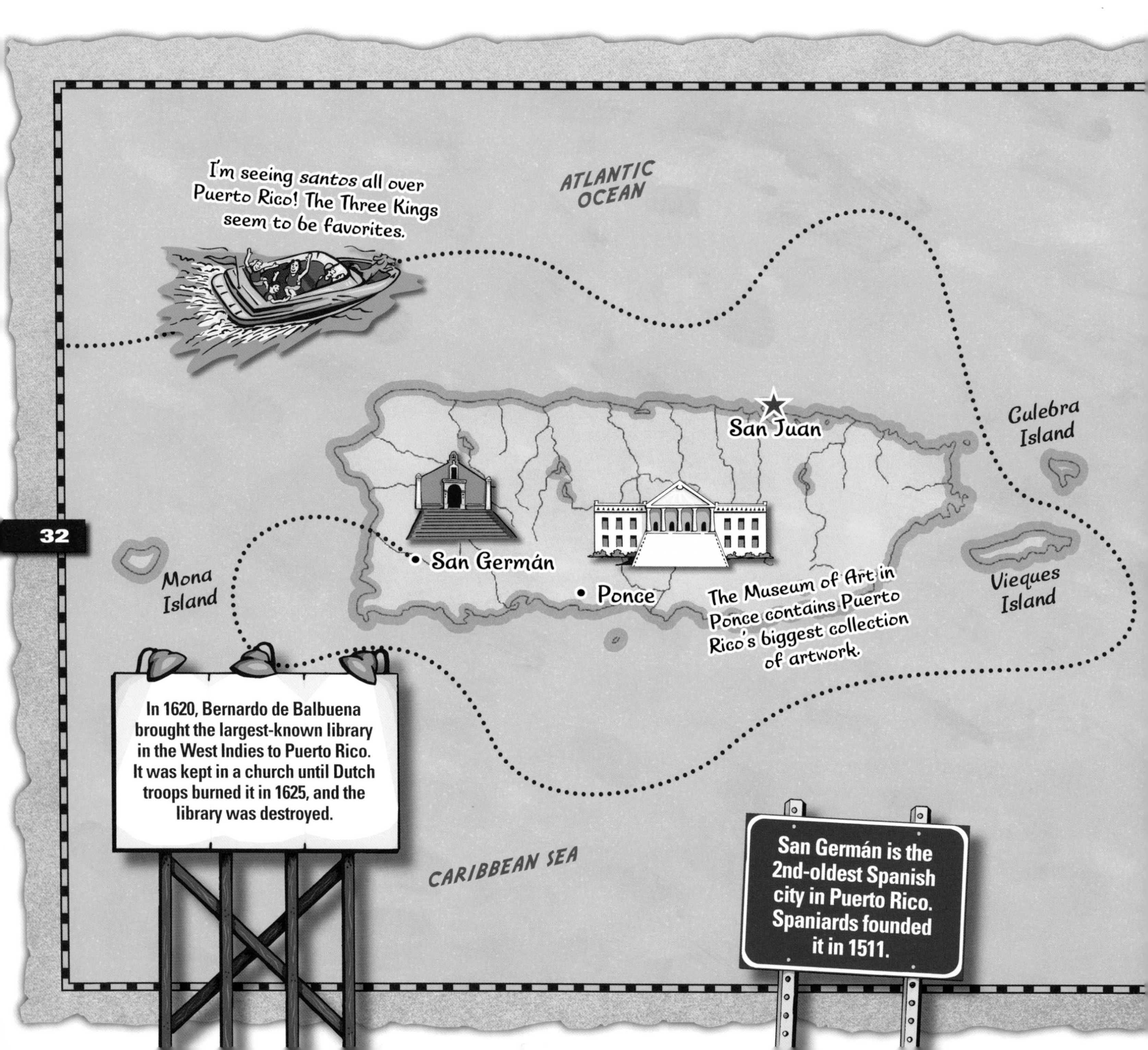

I'm seeing santos all over Puerto Rico! The Three Kings seem to be favorites.
ATLANTIC OCEAN
San Juan
Culebra Island
San Germán
Ponce
Mona Island
Vieques Island
The Museum of Art in Ponce contains Puerto Rico's biggest collection of artwork.
In 1620, Bernardo de Balbuena brought the largest-known library in the West Indies to Puerto Rico. It was kept in a church until Dutch troops burned it in 1625, and the library was destroyed.
CARIBBEAN SEA
San Germán is the 2nd-oldest Spanish city in Puerto Rico. Spaniards founded it in 1511.

Saints at the Gate of Heaven

Wander through the streets of San Germán. Climb the church steps to Porta Coeli. That means "Gate of Heaven"!

This old church was built in 1606. It's now a museum of religious art. There you'll see a display of *santos.* These are saints and other religious figures. Each one is hand-carved from wood.

Carving santos is a fine Puerto Rican craft. Artists who carve them are called *santeros.* Many craftspeople also carve roosters and other birds. Some people weave hammocks. The Taíno Indians began this tradition.

Puerto Rican artist José Campeche painted the art above Porta Coeli's altar.

Visit the beautiful Porta Coeli. You'll see an amazing collection of religious art.

The Capilla del Cristo in Old San Juan displays a large collection of santos.

Take in the beautiful ocean view at Maunabo Lighthouse.

Maunabo Lighthouse

Stroll down to Maunabo Lighthouse. It's right on the coast near Maunabo. You'll see why a lighthouse was built here. The waters are choppy along this rocky coast. The lighthouse blinks a bright signal. It warns ships to stay away from the shore.

Many other lighthouses stand along the coast. Some are still flashing their signals. And a few even have museums.

Spaniards built these lighthouses in the 1800s. Ship traffic was much heavier then. Why not visit a lighthouse? Just watch out for those crashing waves!

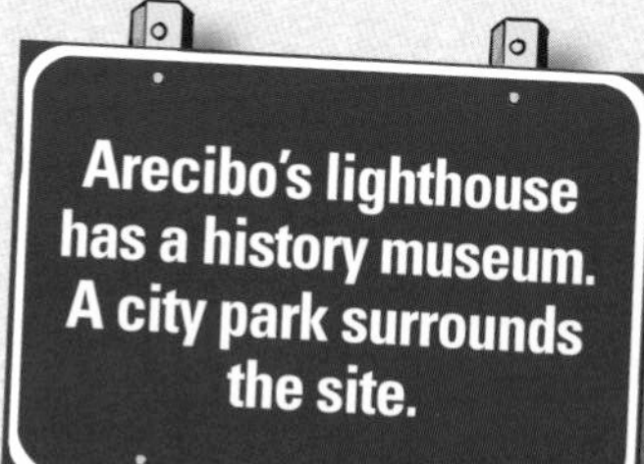

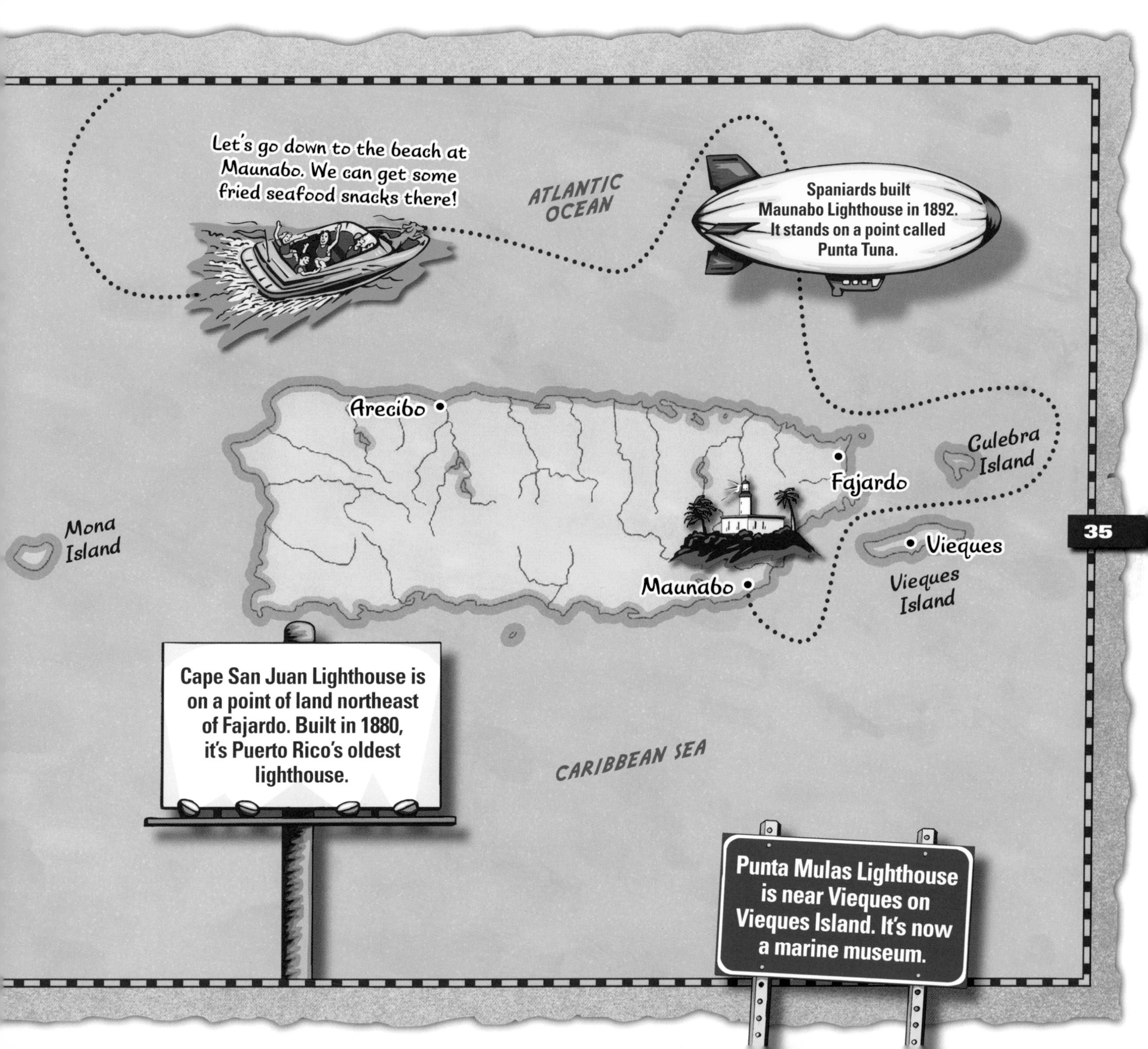
Let's go down to the beach at Maunabo. We can get some fried seafood snacks there!
ATLANTIC OCEAN
Spaniards built Maunabo Lighthouse in 1892. It stands on a point called Punta Tuna.
Arecibo
Culebra Island
Fajardo
Mona Island
Vieques
Maunabo
Vieques Island
Cape San Juan Lighthouse is on a point of land northeast of Fajardo. Built in 1880, it's Puerto Rico's oldest lighthouse.
CARIBBEAN SEA
Punta Mulas Lighthouse is near Vieques on Vieques Island. It's now a marine museum.

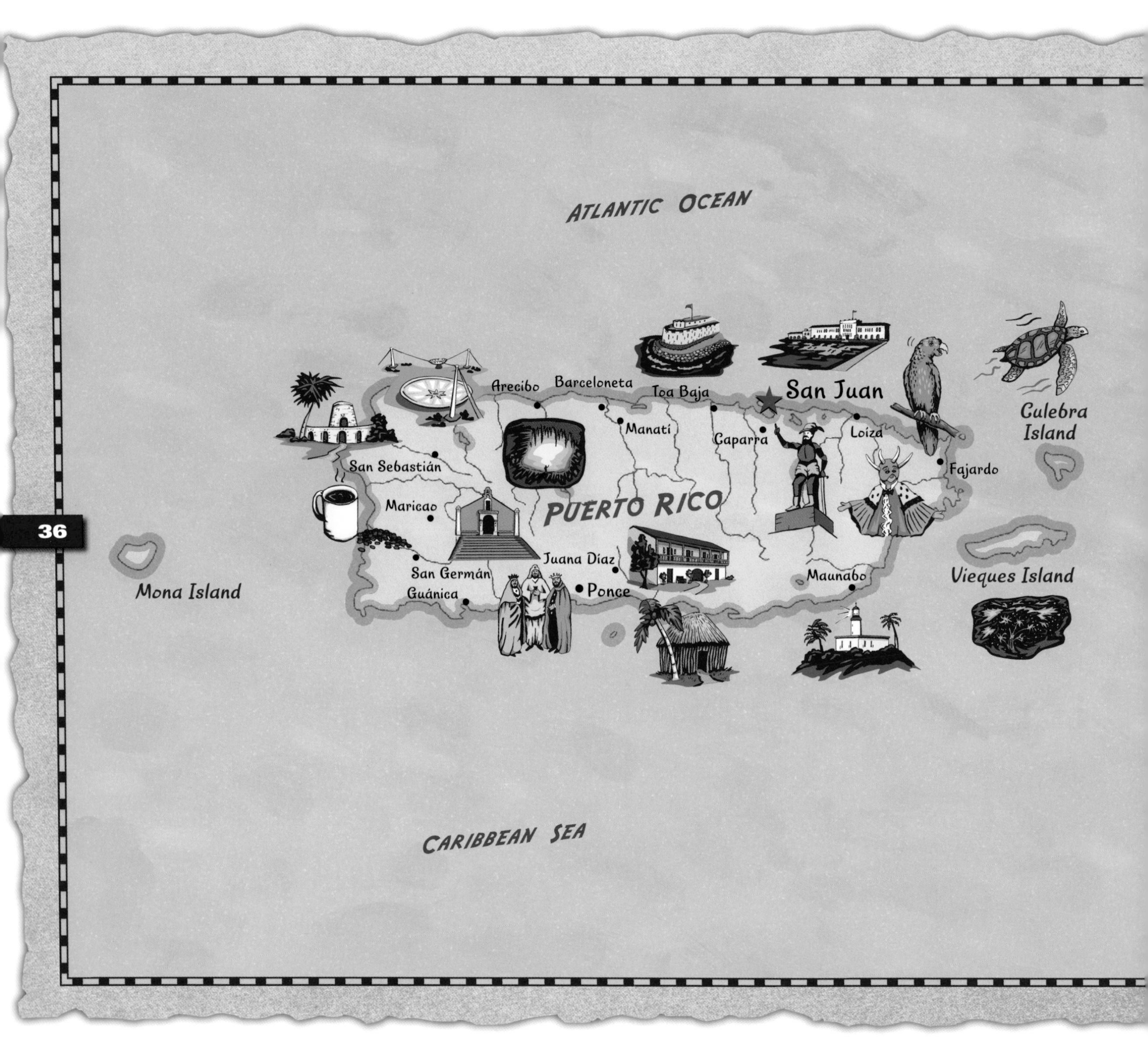
ATLANTIC OCEAN
Arecibo
Barceloneta
Toa Baja
San Juan
Manatí
Caparra
Loíza
Culebra Island
San Sebastián
Fajardo
Maricao
PUERTO RICO
Juana Díaz
San Germán
Maunabo
Vieques Island
Mona Island
Guánica
Ponce
CARIBBEAN SEA

OUR TRIP

We visited many amazing places on our trip! We also met a lot of interesting people along the way. Look at the map on the left. Use your finger to trace all the places we have been.

What is a sinkhole? See page 6 for the answer.

What are Puerto Rico's major small islands? See page 7 for the answer.

Why was the mongoose brought to Puerto Rico? See page 9 for the answer.

What do fireflies and jellyfish have in common? See page 10 for the answer.

What Taino words are used in the English language? See page 12 for the answer.

When did the 1st African slaves arrive in Puerto Rico? See page 14 for the answer.

What are Puerto Rico's official languages? See page 22 for the answer.

Who was Roberto Clemente? See page 31 for the answer.

That was a great trip! We have traveled all over Puerto Rico!

There were a few places we didn't have time for, though. Next time, we plan to visit Culebra National Wildlife Refuge on Culebra Island. Two types of sea turtles make their nests on the refuge. Visitors can hike, bird-watch, and take pictures of the diverse nature.

More Places to Visit in Puerto Rico

WORDS TO KNOW

colonists (KOL-uh-nists) people who settle a new land for their home country

colony (KOL-uh-nee) a land settled and governed by another country

commonwealth (KOM-uhn-welth) name for a state, country, or group of nations; also, a territory tied to the United States but having self-government

culture (KUL-chur) a people's beliefs, customs, and way of life

extra-terrestrial (X-truh tur-RES-tree-uhl) from outer space

industrial (in-DUH-stree-uhl) having to do with businesses and factories

mansion (MAN-shuhn) a large, elegant house

patron saint (PAY-truhn SAYNT) a saint who has a special meaning to a certain group of people

plantations (plan-TAY-shuhnz) large farms that usually raise 1 main crop

rain forest (RAYN FOR-uhst) a forest that gets very heavy rainfall and has tall, broad-leaved evergreen trees

traditions (truh-DISH-uhnz) long-held customs

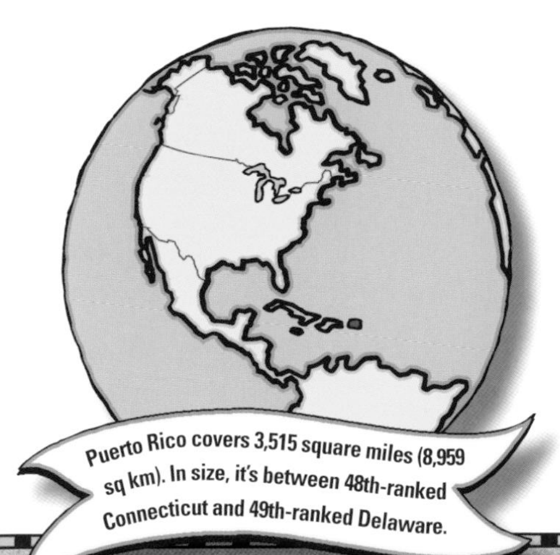

OFFICIAL SYMBOLS

Official bird: Reina mora (stripe-headed tanager)

Official flower: Flor de maga (Puerto Rican hibiscus)

Official tree: Ceiba (silk-cotton tree)

Popular animal symbol: Coquí (tree frog)

Official Flag

Official Seal

OFFICIAL SONG

"La Borinqueña"

Original words and music by Felix Astol y Artés; new words by Manuel Fernández Juncos; new musical arrangement by Ramón Collado

Spanish:

La tierra de Borinquen
donde he nacido yo,
es un jardín florido
de mágico fulgor.

Un cielo siempre nítido
le sirve de dosel
y dan arrullos plácidos
las olas a sus pies.

Cuando a sus playas llegó Colón;
Exclamó lleno de admiración;
"Oh!, oh!, oh!, esta es la linda
tierra que busco yo."

Es Borinquen la hija,
la hija del mar y el sol,
del mar y el sol,
del mar y el sol,
del mar y el sol,
del mar y el sol.

English:

The land of Borinquen
where I have been born,
It is a florid garden
of magical brilliance.

A sky always clean
serves as a canopy,
And placid lullabies are given
by the waves at her feet.

When at her beaches Columbus
arrived,
he exclaimed full of admiration:
"Oh! Oh! Oh!
This is the beautiful land that I seek."

It is Borinquen the daughter,
the daughter of the sea and the sun,
of the sea and the sun,
of the sea and the sun,
of the sea and the sun,
of the sea and the sun!

FAMOUS PEOPLE

Albizu Campos, Pedro (1893-1965), political activist

Barbosa, José Celso (1857-1921), politician

Burgos, Julia de (1914-1953), poet

Campeche, José (1751-1809), painter

Clemente, Roberto (1934-1972), baseball player

Del Toro, Benicio (1967-), actor

Feliciano, José (1945-), singer and guitarist

Ferrer, José (1909-1992), actor

Julia, Raul (1940-1994), actor

Martin, Ricky (1971-), singer

Moreno, Rita (1931-), actor and singer

Muñoz Marín, Luis (1898-1980), politician

Puente, Tito (1923-2000), musician

Rivera, Chita (1933-), dancer and actor

Rivera, Geraldo (1943-), journalist

Ruiz Belvis, Segundo (1829-1867), abolitionist

Smits, Jimmy (1955-), actor

Torres, Edwin (1931-), judge and author

Trinidad, Tito (1973-), boxer

TO FIND OUT MORE

At the Library

Bernier-Grand, Carmen T., and Ernesto Ramos Nieves (illustrator). *Juan Bobo: Four Folktales from Puerto Rico.* New York: Harper Collins, 1994.

George, Linda, and Charles George. *Luis Muñoz Marín: Father of Modern Puerto Rico.* New York: Children's Press, 1999.

Olmstead, Mary. *Roberto Clemente.* Chicago: Raintree, 2004.

Olmstead, Mary. *Tito Puente.* Chicago: Raintree, 2004.

Ramirez, Michael Rose, and Margaret Sanfilippo (illustrator). *The Legend of the Hummingbird: A Tale from Puerto Rico.* Greenvale, N.Y.: Mondo, 1998.

On the Web

Visit our home page for lots of links about Puerto Rico:
http://www.childsworld.com/links

Note to Parents, Teachers, and Librarians: We routinely verify our Web links to make sure they are safe, active sites—so encourage your readers to check them out!

Places to Visit or Contact

Institute of Puerto Rican Culture
Section 9024184
San Juan, Puerto Rico 00902
787/724-0700
For more information about the history of Puerto Rico

Puerto Rico Tourism Company
La Princesa Building #2 Paseo La Princesa
Old San Juan, Puerto Rico 00902
800/866-7827
For more information about traveling in Puerto Rico

INDEX

Bye, Isle of Enchantment.
We had a great time.
We'll come back soon!